Eddie Obeng's

SOUND**BYTES**

*Creative stimuli for your
New World*

PENTACLE WORKS
THE VIRTUAL MEDIA COMPANY

First Published 1999 by
Pentacle Works
Burke Lodge
20 London End
Beaconsfield
Bucks HP9 2JH
http://www.pentaclethevbs.com

British Library
Cataloguing in Publication Data
A CIP catalogue record for this book is
available from the British Library

ISBN 0 9534869 0 7

Design and typesetting by
Sparks Computer Solutions
The Oxford Enterprise Centre
Cave Street
Oxford OX4 1BA
http://www.sparks.co.uk

Illustrated by Sparks Computer Solutions
and Richard Wise
Cover design by Richard Wise

Printed and bound at
The University Press, Cambridge

HOW THIS BOOK CAME ABOUT

A while ago, after one of my conference keynote presentations, one of the participants came up to me and said 'I really loved your one-liners. They kept sparking off ideas In my head, like fireworks. I spent all my time jotting them down. I didn't really have a chance to listen to what else you said. Sometimes with the pressures of getting things done, I get stuck and just the right quote can give me the breakthrough I need. Also, where I find them really useful is in meetings or presentation, I need just the right saying or quote to light the bulbs in my team or managers' minds to encapsulate a point.' I smiled at the time and thanked her; I couldn't think of a suitable response.

Shortly after, at another conference where copies of one of my books were being handed out, I wanted to make the point that it was possible to make even commodity products valuable by individual tailoring. So I personally signed each book, including in it a unique and personalising '*soundbyte*'. This transformed the books from identical products to unique and rare specimens. At the conference I first got the delegates to read the quote I had written 'specifically' for them and then suggested that people swap at random with someone sitting close by. Not surprisingly, no one swapped.

A *Soundbyte* is a clear, distinct, quotable piece of information that I have learnt and use. Unlike a *soundbite* which is often vacuous, a *Soundbyte* contains good, New World common sense.

The soundbytes in this book are 'one-liners' I use myself to tackle the New World's opportunities and challenges. Anyone who knows me well will recognise my favourites – 'that's really Old World', 'see you in cyberspace', 'one step at a time' and 'beware the money making machine'.

(Now for my Oscars ceremony speech.) I'd like to thank Franck –my alter-ego – for many of these *Soundbytes*. My other books are written as part-businesss-novel, containing ~~real~~ fictional cases (which cut through the window dressing and get to the heart of the issues real people face in real organisations) and as part handbook/working framework/text book/reference book. The common thread across a wide range of topics is the character Franck, a full-time know-it-all, and not always helpful inquisitor whom you may have come across in the books *New Rules for the New World – Cautionary Tales for the New World Manager, All Change! The Project Leader's Secret Handbook, Putting Strategy to Work – The Blueprint for Transforming Ideas into Action, Making Re-engineering Happen – What's Wrong with the Organisation Anyway?, Cybersense!* and *Achieving Organisational Magic.* Franck first spoke many of these *Soundbytes* with his drawl. Let's hear it for Franck! And now, another thunderous round of applause for Susan, my inspiration and love.

Seven of the one hundred and forty-three *Soundbytes* included here, I know I learnt from someone else, but I use them so often that they have become part of me.

I hope *Soundbytes* provides you with inspiration, fun and learning.

Dr Eddie Obeng
Burke Lodge
September 1998

HOW TO USE THIS BOOK

This amazing little book will help you through any New World paradox, leadership crossroads or personal vision crisis.

Simply hold the paradox or problem firmly in your mind, close your eyes, relax, breathe slowly and rhythmically, and then pick up and open the book at random.

You will find it opens at a page which provides a unique insight, and allows you to leap from the clutches of your paradox.

As a non-optional extra this book will provide just the right New World quote for your presentation, meeting, interview, negotiation or sales deal.

Enjoy.

eddie.obeng@pentaclethevbs.com

The buzz

Handling change

Leading people

Feeling confident

The cyberPioneer

Pick 'n' mix

THE
BUZZ

The future is NOW...
because most of us
are already late!

Don't be a leader – become an organisational magician!

3

Focus! Focus Frequently!

Seek what you do not
already know when you do
not yet need it!

Manage change in chunks
and hold on to your gains.

The present is the
most probable route
out of the past.

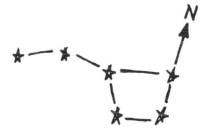

The more you give away
the more you get:
information!

To us, the distinction between past,
present and future is only an illusion,
if a somewhat stubborn one..

(borrowed from Einstein)

Sometimes,
The New World
just won't wait!

Respond with
awesome
velocity.

The joy of having
constraints is that there
are never many of them.
It is rare to find a
really complex problem
with more than half a
dozen real constraints.

Processes, Projects,
Programs always cost
money. All work costs
money. Thank goodness
for the customers who
generously give it back.

13

Question to ask in a
shop selling money
making machines –
"Which machine makes
money fastest?"

Change and Improvement
are not the same thing!

Loop up the money:
co-evolve with your
customers.

CHUNK IT OR JUNK IT!

(borrowed from Gareth Jones)

The timing of communication must anticipate the thoughts and actions of the person being communicated with.

Strategy is the
continuous manipulation
of our future.

19

Make time fit!

Show me the money!

To make money now and in the future you must: concentrate on doing better what you do today. To make money now and in the future you must: concentrate on doing something different for tomorrow.

On the Internet, no one knows if you're a dog
(*borrowed anon*)

The New World makes
babies of us all!

Go for it!

LEADING
PEOPLE

The followers
determine the leader.
The determination of
the leader,
leads to followers.

In the New World Leadership
comes from the front —
Not always the same
as the top!

29

Emotion first,
logic second ...
human design.

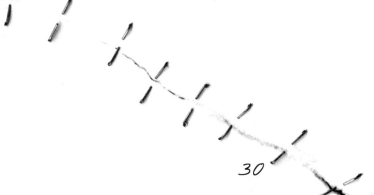

Perspective, use it —
or lose it.
(borrowed from
Richard Bach)

In a self directed team,
actions are carried out
even though no orders are
given!

Focus on improving today
AND on creating tomorrow

33

Sometimes the most
effective leaders
are invisible!

Build your own unique
cyberpersonality.

35

The human being is an
amazing animal —
capable of the greatest
good — and greatest evil —
capable of grand vision and
Luddite myopia ...
Most of the people I know
are human beings.

There is no point in
tackling anything except
the root cause!

Copy everyone.
I imitate no-one.

The job of the organisational
magician is to breathe life
into the virtual organisation.

Simultaneously gain and
store perspective ...

40

See yourself as creator –
enabler rather than
driver-conqueror!

In the Fog –
without trust,
there is no leadership.

You can't have
organisational leadership
without thought leadership.

43

Confronted with change,
people's first reaction is
emotional and then, if
you're lucky, they move
into the logical phase.

Go into the future to
find out the effects of
your actions. Go into
the past and review.

45

Trust first,
then tit-for-tat.

Unbalance your team in the
direction of your change!

47

*Strategic change is weird,
strategic change is different –
with strategic change you may
never experience the full effect
of your actions!*

Sometimes wizardry is more useful than leadership!

49

Change DEPENDENCE to INTERDEPENDENCE

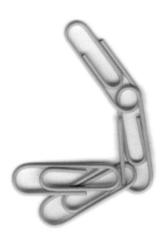

I'm sure if you were right
I'd agree with you.

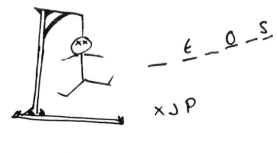

_ E _ _ O _ S

X J P

51

Assume FAIR = DIFFERENT,
not FAIR = EQUAL.

There is no problem so big it cannot be
run away from!

(borrowed from Snoopy the Dog)

Manage complexity and
avoid complication.

Sometimes the "Pattern"
is all you have
(... and you wish you'd
seen it before ...)

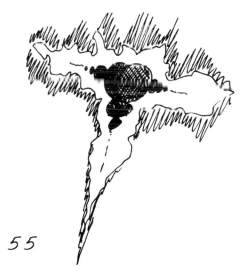

55

After all ... You can't HEAR
laughter in Cyberspace!

HANDLING CHANGE

Beware the
Money Making Machine!

58

Don't change anything!

Handling
change

Beware the
LAWS OF CHANGE.

Without Change there is
no Outcome.

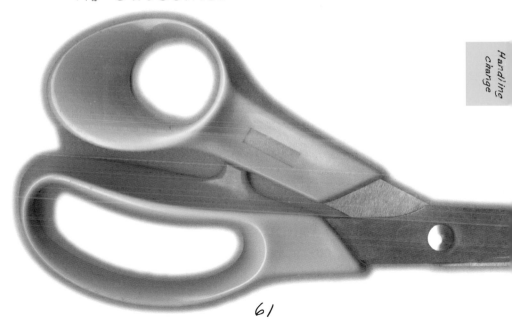

61

Why?

62

The more successful an organisation has been in the past the more in need of re-engineering it is likely to be — especially if its success is based on a tried and tested recipe.

Eddie Obeng's "Laws of Change"

I One change leads to another!

If creating the world took six days, then how come changing it takes longer?

Eddie Obeng's "Laws of Change"

II Adding change to change creates chaos!

Success is not the result of one day or event. Nor is failure the result of one day or event. Both success and failure come from gradual development!

Eddie Obeng's "Laws of Change"

I I I People create change.
People constrain change!

Stakeholders rule OK!

Handling
charge

"That's really Old World."

Eddie Obeng's "Laws of Change"

IV Accomplished change is change chosen and carried out carefully.

71

"It's the people,
stoopid!"

It takes all the running you can do to stay in the same place.

(The Red Queen Hypothesis, borrowed from Lewis Carroll.)

Eddie Obeng's "Laws of Change"

V *The challenge of creating change is the opposite of the amount of accumulated complacency.*

Big change in chunks –
loosely coupled but
tightly aligned.

However complex the situation
it is unusual to find more
than half a dozen underlying
causes!

Eddie Obeng's "Laws of Change"

VI. Resistance to change accumulates over time — and the cumulative change can't be carried out all at once.

It's about changing anything which provides a block to improving today's business performance – even if it means going back to the drawing board!

Manage your change
in "Chunks".

Every group a culture.

Make it self-similar.

81

Old route from Reality to Vision

- create B
- consider A
- create a route from A to B

New route from Vision to Reality

- create (a constantly changing) B
- work backward through time
- re-create A now!

The stakeholders determine the success of the change.

Work "Back from the Future".

Everything has sell-by dates.

Eggs ~~£1.15~~ {Got}
Bread
Cash for Sat
lemons.

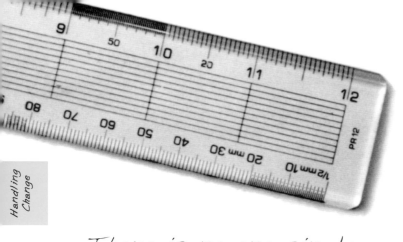

There is no one single
BEST process.

86

<Selection method to replacer the old world job related; Tinker, Tailor, Soldier, Sailor, Rich man, Poor man, Beggar man, Thief>

Tinker, Tidy, Re-engineer, Release, Improve, Design, Re-invent, Create.

Sometimes the soft stuff is harder.

Learn to communicate Purpose.

89

Say "AND!" not "OR".

The drumbeat absorbs
the chaos of change.

FEELING
CONFIDENT

One step at a time.

94

Sometimes the follower
is braver than the leader.

95

Go into the future
and find out.

Everything is invented twice -
first in the mind!
(borrowed from Albert Einstein)

97

You have probably already done it!

An ability to see emergent future patterns is more useful in business than horse racing.

99

Those who do not learn from the
past are condemned to ... (add
those mistakes to the ones that
they are making now!)

Don't eat the menu!

Go confidently in
the direction of
your dreams!
(*borrowed anon.*)

Deep within each of us, often forgotten, is a reserve of courage — a lake big enough to make us immortal heroes and heroines.

Sometimes you have to
discover it for yourself.

104

Only learn what
others don't know!

105

Unlearn EVERYTHING!

106

Review too often!

In the New World it makes
sense to predict potential
problems, so that you do not
have to live through them.

Do it Now!

109

Delight and Challenge
the people you work with.

DO IT ONCE.

111

Split Accountability from
Responsibility.

feeling
confident

112

Personal Change is best handled
by re- inventing your microhabits!

113

Pentacle's money making machine

1   Will this change help us make money faster now or in the future?

Pentacle's money making machine

2   Will this change reduce the rate at which we have to spend money to operate, now or in the future?

Pentacle's money making machine

3   Will this change release money tied up in the business?

Pentacle's money making machine

4   Does this change help us to meet
(externally imposed) necessary conditions?

Onward and upward.

THE
CYBERPIONEER

Grow your cyberpersonality. It's the only thing your virtual friends will notice!

Communicate to serve the
purpose of the person being
communicated with.

Sometimes Sane People talk to themselves!

Being virtual ... having the same effect without the traditional form.

GO VIRTUAL!

Data, Data everywhere ...
but not a drop of information.

Don't mistake the process of making money with the process for controlling spending it!

$£7.11$

$15p$

7.26

$= £3.63$ each

126

The structure of the organisation no longer needs to be the same as the information flow or reporting structure.

... People working together ...

A new world riddle. What is it that – the more I give away the more I have? The more I sell the more I have to sell? The more I use it the less I have to use it?

<What answer is this the question to?>

Information.

<What question is this the answer to?>

HEADACHE!

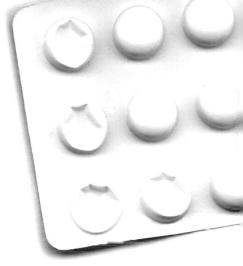

Stop communicating!

Stay *DIGITAL* in Cyberspace.

ALL CONSTRAINTS INTO
TOUCHSPACE.

Modularize!

Who is standing on the sidelines
betting on your success?

135

Information and data are
NOT the same,
information is the answer
to the question asked.

Some suppliers are more
important than some customers.

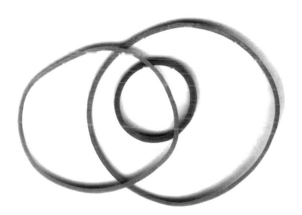

137

Do NOTHING which is of NO use.

In Cyberspace no one can hear you scream! (And they can ignore your emails even if you ask for a receipt.)

Cyberspace – the final frontier!

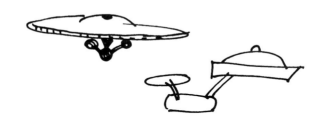

140

Bet on teams AND networks AND the individual.

Develop more styles.

142

Change the world (Old to New).

... fun and learning
(borrowed from R. Bach).

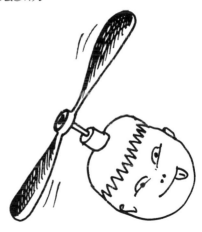

145

Know your stakeholders ...
if you ignore them they
always come back and
"bite your bum".

146

Make TIME = PARALLEL.

147

Re-invent your information.

148

How?

Always "anchor" virtuous cycles!

150

Focus!

Pick 'n' mix

Robust or Bust!

152

Co-evolve!
... but take care of who
you choose to co-evolve with.

Paradox busting – Zap them now
... imagine a world where all goals
and conditions are met.

Time is sometimes best
folded in on itself.

Stick to the organisational drumbeat ... and you will all have a great jamming session.

Remember to
- identify your constraints first
- fully utilise the constraints
- support and only support your constraints
- improve and alleviate your constraints
- look for your new constraints and repeat.

(borrowed from Eli Goldratt.)

Seize the future,
Now!

See you in cyberspace

eddie.obeng@pentaclethevbs.com

Dr Eddie Obeng

BURKE LODGE, 20 LONDON END, BEACONSFIELD, BUCKINGHAMSHIRE, HP9 2JH
VOICE 01494 678555, MOBILE 0831 826168, FAX 01494 671291
E MAIL 100071.513, @ COMPUSERVE.COM CIX ID: FRANCK

159